EAT THAT FROG!

21 GREAT WAYS TO STOP PROCRASTINATING AND GET MORE DONE IN LESS TIME

from SmarterComics

BRIAN TRACY

EAT THAT FROG!

21 GREAT WAYS TO STOP PROCRASTINATING AND GET MORE DONE IN LESS TIME

from SmarterComics

BRIAN TRACY

Paul Maybury	Illustrator
Gabriel Bautista	Lettering
Cullen Bunn	Script
D.J. Kirbride	Editor
Jennifer Kunz	Creative Director
Sander Pieterse	Designer
Franco Arda	CEO SmarterComics

Printed in Canada

ISBN-13: 9781610820028

FOREWORD

Dear friends,

Are you procrastinating? You're not alone. In a busy age of tweets, posts, emails and instant messages, it can be difficult to effectively manage your tasks. Unfortunately, the information deluge isn't going to stop anytime soon: it's up to you to find a strategy that allows you to fully participate in our modern world without getting behind on your work.

That's why you're holding the SmarterComics version of my best-selling book, "EAT THAT FROG! 21 Great Ways to Stop Procrastinating and Get More Done in Less Time." Thanks to this book, millions of people have learned how to stop stalling and start making it happen, no matter how overwhelming their lives may be. Now, through the visual power of comics, this book is even easier and faster to read. You can absorb all the key points on getting your task management under control while checking out the beautifully illustrated panels. Learning how not to procrastinate has never been so fun.

Whether you only have time for a quick read or an in-depth perusal, this SmarterComics version will help you get more done in shorter amounts of time. By developing a whole new way of conceptualizing of work, strategy, and focus, you can kick old habits and start tackling your day with energy and purpose. Better yet, you can pick up these procrastination-busting techniques in under an hour. The streamlined, graphically arresting format makes this book fun to read and easy to remember. You can read it in a physical book format, or download the App for your iPhone, iPad or Android. Result: no matter where you go, you can read up on these incredible techniques on the fly.

Now how cool is that?

Brian Tracy

THE SECOND RULE OF FROG EATING IS: IF YOU HAVE TO EAT A LIVE FROG AT ALL, IT DOESN'T PAY TO SIT AND LOOK AT IT FOR VERY LONG.

THE KEY TO REACHING HIGH LEVELS OF PERFORMANCE AND PRODUCTIVITY IS TO DEVELOP THE LIFELONG HABIT OF TACKLING YOUR MAJOR TASKS *FIRST THING* EACH MORNING.

YOU MUST DEVELOP THE ROUTINE OF EATING YOUR FROG BEFORE YOU DO ANYTHING ELSE, WITHOUT TAKING TOO MUCH TIME TO THINK ABOUT IT.

"FAILURE TO EXECUTE" IS ONE OF THE BIGGEST PROBLEMS IN ORGANIZATIONS TODAY.

MANY PEOPLE CONFUSE *ACTIVITY* WITH *ACCOMPLISHMENT*.

THEY TALK CONTINUOUSLY, HOLD ENDLESS MEETINGS, AND MAKE WONDERFUL PLANS -- BUT IN THE FINAL ANALYSIS, NO ONE DOES THE JOB AND GETS THE REQUIRED RESULTS.

YOUR SUCCESS IN LIFE AND WORK WILL BE DETERMINED BY THE KINDS OF HABITS YOU DEVELOP OVER TIME.

THE HABIT OF SETTING PRIORITIES, OVERCOMING PROCRASTINATION, AND GETTING ON WITH YOUR MOST IMPORTANT TASK IS A MENTAL AND PHYSICAL SKILL.

THE HABIT OF STARTING AND COMPLETING IMPORTANT TASKS HAS AN IMMEDIATE AND CONTINUOUS PAYOFF.

TO-DO LIST

THE COMPLETION OF AN IMPORTANT TASK TRIGGERS THE RELEASE OF ENDORPHINS IN YOUR BRAIN.

WHENEVER YOU COMPLETE A TASK OF ANY SIZE OR IMPORTANCE, YOU FEEL A SURGE OF ENERGY, ENTHUSIASM, AND SELF-ESTEEM.

THE ENDORPHIN RUSH THAT FOLLOWS THE SUCCESSFUL COMPLETION OF A TASK MAKES YOU FEEL MORE POSITIVE, PERSONABLE, CREATIVE, AND CONFIDENT.

HERE IS ONE OF THE MOST IMPORTANT OF THE SO-CALLED SECRETS OF SUCCESS:

YOU CAN DEVELOP A "POSITIVE ADDICTION" TO ENDORPHINS AND TO THE FEELINGS OF ENHANCED CLARITY, CONFIDENCE, AND COMPETENCE THEY TRIGGER.

ONE OF THE KEYS TO LIVING A WONDERFUL LIFE AND FEELING TERRIFIC ABOUT YOURSELF IS TO DEVELOP THE HABIT OF STARTING AND FINISHING IMPORTANT JOBS.

WHEN YOU DO, THIS BEHAVIOR WILL TAKE ON A POWER OF ITS OWN! YOU'LL FIND IT *EASIER* TO COMPLETE IMPORTANT TASKS THAN TO *NOT* COMPLETE THEM.

THERE IS A SPECIAL WAY YOU CAN ACCELERATE YOUR PROGRESS TOWARD BECOMING THE HIGHLY PRODUCTIVE, EFFECTIVE, AND EFFICIENT PERSON YOU WANT TO BE.

IT CONSISTS OF YOU CONTINUALLY THINKING ABOUT THE REWARDS AND BENEFITS OF BEING AN ACTION-ORIENTED, FAST-MOVING, AND FOCUSED PERSON.

SEE YOURSELF AS THE KIND OF PERSON WHO GETS IMPORTANT JOBS DONE QUICKLY AND WELL ON A CONSISTENT BASIS.

YOU HAVE A VIRTUALLY UNLIMITED ABILITY TO LEARN AND DEVELOP NEW SKILLS AND HABITS.

WHEN YOU TRAIN YOURSELF TO OVERCOME PROCRASTINATION AND GET THE MOST IMPORTANT TASKS COMPLETED QUICKLY, YOU WILL MOVE YOURSELF ONTO THE FAST TRACK IN YOUR LIFE AND CAREER.

BEFORE YOU DETERMINE YOUR "FROG" AND GET ON WITH THE JOB OF EATING IT, YOU HAVE TO DECIDE EXACTLY WHAT YOU WANT TO ACHIEVE IN EACH AREA OF YOUR LIFE.

CLARITY IS PERHAPS THE MOST IMPORTANT CONCEPT IN PERSONAL PRODUCTIVITY.

THE GREATER THE CLARITY YOU HAVE REGARDING WHAT YOU WANT AND THE STEPS YOU MUST TAKE TO ACHIEVE IT...

...THE EASIER IT WILL BE FOR YOU TO OVERCOME PROCRASTINATION, EAT YOUR FROG, AND COMPLETE THE TASK AT HAND.

THE MAJOR REASON FOR PROCRASTINATION AND LACK OF MOTIVATION ARE VAGUENESS, CONFUSION, AND FUZZY-MINDEDNESS ABOUT WHAT YOU ARE TRYING TO DO AND IN WHAT ORDER AND FOR WHAT REASON.

THERE IS A POWERFUL FORMULA FOR SETTING AND ACHIEVING GOALS THAT YOU CAN USE FOR THE REST OF YOUR LIFE.

IT CONSISTS OF SEVEN SIMPLE STEPS.

7

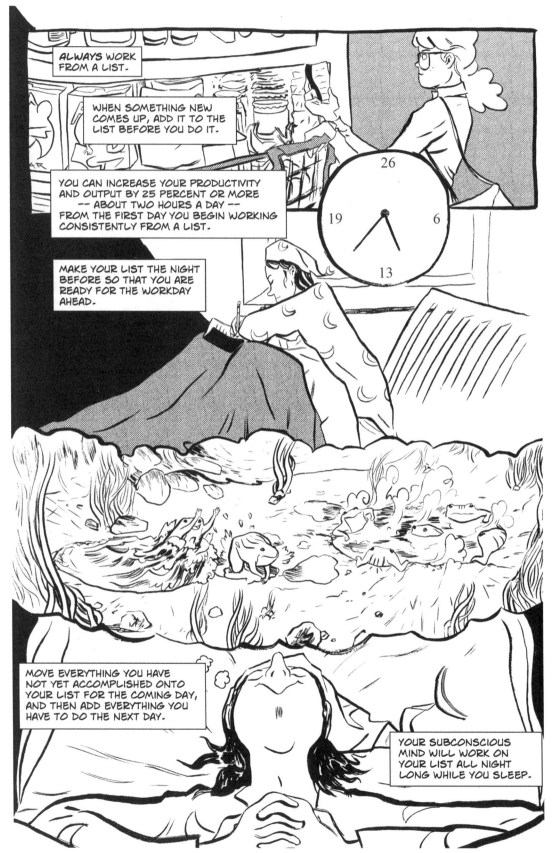

ALWAYS WORK FROM A LIST.

WHEN SOMETHING NEW COMES UP, ADD IT TO THE LIST BEFORE YOU DO IT.

YOU CAN INCREASE YOUR PRODUCTIVITY AND OUTPUT BY 25 PERCENT OR MORE -- ABOUT TWO HOURS A DAY -- FROM THE FIRST DAY YOU BEGIN WORKING CONSISTENTLY FROM A LIST.

MAKE YOUR LIST THE NIGHT BEFORE SO THAT YOU ARE READY FOR THE WORKDAY AHEAD.

MOVE EVERYTHING YOU HAVE NOT YET ACCOMPLISHED ONTO YOUR LIST FOR THE COMING DAY, AND THEN ADD EVERYTHING YOU HAVE TO DO THE NEXT DAY.

YOUR SUBCONSCIOUS MIND WILL WORK ON YOUR LIST ALL NIGHT LONG WHILE YOU SLEEP.

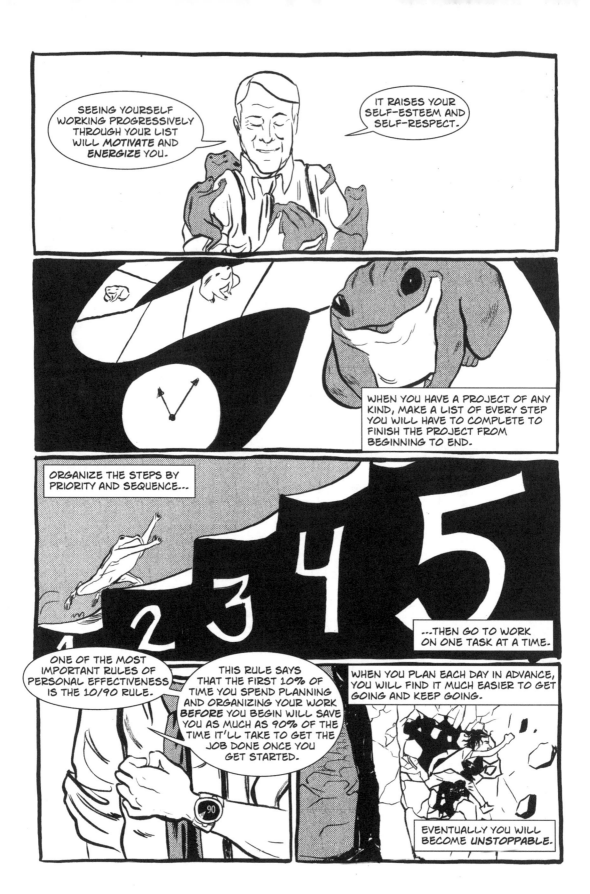

THE HARDEST PART OF ANY IMPORTANT TASK IS GETTING STARTED ON IT IN THE FIRST PLACE.

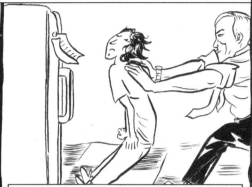

ONCE YOU ACTUALLY BEGIN WORK ON A VALUABLE TASK, YOU WILL BE NATURALLY MOTIVATED TO CONTINUE.

TIME MANAGEMENT IS REALLY *LIFE MANAGEMENT*, PERSONAL MANAGEMENT.

IT IS REALLY TAKING CONTROL OF THE *SEQUENCE OF EVENTS*.

YOUR ABILITY TO CHOOSE BETWEEN THE IMPORTANT AND THE UNIMPORTANT IS THE KEY DETERMINANT OF YOUR SUCCESS IN LIFE AND WORK.

EFFECTIVE, PRODUCTIVE PEOPLE DISCIPLINE THEMSELVES TO START ON THE MOST IMPORTANT TASKS *FIRST*.

URGENT

THEY FORCE THEMSELVES TO EAT THAT FROG -- WHATEVER IT IS.

THE MARK OF THE SUPERIOR THINKER IS THE ABILITY TO ACCURATELY PREDICT THE CONSEQUENCES OF DOING OR NOT DOING SOMETHING.

THE POTENTIAL CONSEQUENCES OF ANY TASK OR ACTIVITY ARE THE KEY DETERMINANTS OF HOW IMPORTANT A TASK REALLY IS TO YOU AND YOUR COMPANY.

YOUR ATTITUDE TOWARD TIME, YOUR "TIME HORIZON," HAS AN ENORMOUS IMPACT ON YOUR BEHAVIOR AND YOUR CHOICES.

LONG-TERM THINKING IMPROVES SHORT-TERM DECISION-MAKING.

SUCCESSFUL PEOPLE HAVE A CLEAR FUTURE ORIENTATION.

THEY THINK FIVE, TEN, OR EVEN TWENTY YEARS OUT INTO THE FUTURE.

5

0

10

20

SUCCESSFUL PEOPLE ARE THOSE WILLING TO DELAY GRATIFICATION AND MAKE SACRIFICES IN THE SHORT TERM SO THEY CAN ENJOY FAR GREATER REWARDS IN THE LONG TERM.

UNSUCCESSFUL PEOPLE, ON THE OTHER HAND, THINK ABOUT SHORT-TERM PLEASURE AND IMMEDIATE GRATIFICATION WHILE GIVING LITTLE THOUGHT TO THE LONG-TERM FUTURE.

IF A TASK OR ACTIVITY HAS LARGE POTENTIAL POSITIVE CONSEQUENCES, MAKE IT A TOP PRIORITY AND GET STARTED ON IT IMMEDIATELY.

KEEP YOURSELF FOCUSED AND FORWARD MOVING BY CONTINUALLY STARTING AND COMPLETING THOSE TASKS THAT CAN MAKE A MAJOR DIFFERENCE TO YOUR COMPANY AND YOUR FUTURE.

THE LAW OF FORCED EFFICIENCY SAYS THAT "THERE IS NEVER ENOUGH TIME TO DO EVERY-THING, BUT THERE IS ALWAYS ENOUGH TIME TO DO THE MOST IMPORTANT THING.

PUT ANOTHER WAY, YOU CANNOT EAT EVERY FROG IN THE POND...

...BUT YOU CAN EAT THE BIGGEST AND UGLIEST ONE, AND THAT WILL BE ENOUGH, AT LEAST FOR THE TIME BEING.

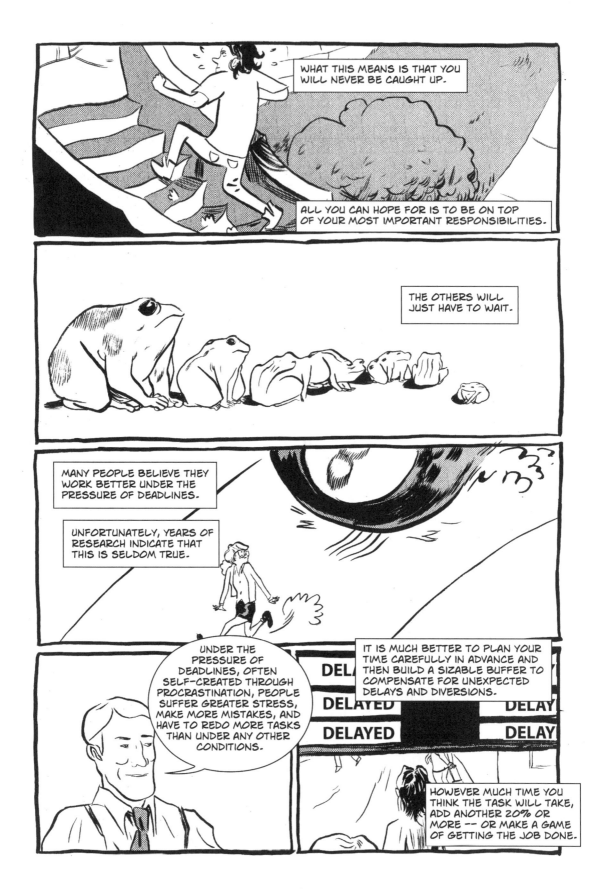

TO SET PRIORITIES...

...YOU MUST SET **POSTERIORITIES** AS WELL.

A PRIORITY IS SOMETHING YOU DO MORE OF AND SOONER...

...WHILE A POSTERIORITY IS SOMETHING YOU DO LESS OF AND LATER, IF AT ALL.

ONE OF THE MOST POWERFUL OF ALL WORDS IN TIME MANAGEMENT IS THE WORD...

NO

SAY **NO** TO ANYTHING THAT IS NOT A HIGH-VALUE USE OF YOUR TIME AND YOUR LIFE.

23

AN "E" TASK IS DEFINED AS SOMETHING YOU CAN ELIMINATE ALTOGETHER, AND IT WON'T MAKE A REAL DIFFERENCE.

EVERY MINUTE YOU SPEND ON AN "E" TASK IS TIME TAKEN AWAY FROM A TASK OR ACTIVITY THAT CAN MAKE A *REAL* DIFFERENCE IN YOUR LIFE.

THE KEY TO MAKING THIS ABCDE METHOD WORK IS FOR YOU TO DISCIPLINE YOURSELF TO START IMMEDIATELY ON YOUR A-1 TASK AND STAY ON IT UNTIL IT IS COMPLETE.

USE YOUR WILLPOWER TO GET GOING AND STAY GOING ON THIS ONE JOB, THE MOST IMPORTANT SINGLE TASK YOU COULD POSSIBLY BE DOING.

EAT THE WHOLE FROG, AND DON'T STOP UNTIL IT'S COMPLETELY FINISHED.

WHEN YOU DEVELOP THE HABIT OF CONCENTRATING ON YOUR A-1 ACTIVITY, YOU WILL START GETTING MORE DONE THAN ANY TWO OR THREE PEOPLE AROUND YOU.

WHY AM I ON THE PAYROLL?

THIS IS ONE OF THE MOST IMPORTANT QUESTIONS YOU CAN EVER ASK AND ANSWER, OVER AND OVER AGAIN, THROUGHOUT YOUR CAREER.

GREG

IF YOU ARE NOT CRYSTAL CLEAR ABOUT WHY YOU ARE ON THE PAYROLL AND WHAT RESULTS YOU HAVE BEEN HIRED TO ACCOMPLISH...

...IT IS VERY HARD FOR YOU TO PERFORM AT YOUR BEST, GET PAID MORE, AND GET PROMOTED FASTER.

YOUR JOB CAN BE BROKEN DOWN INTO ABOUT FIVE TO SEVEN KEY RESULT AREAS, SELDOM MORE.

THESE REPRESENT THE RESULTS YOU WILL ABSOLUTELY, POSITIVELY NEED TO FULFILL YOUR RESPONSIBILITIES AND MAKE YOUR MAXIMUM CONTRIBUTION TO YOUR ORGANIZATION.

A KEY RESULT AREA IS DEFINED AS SOMETHING FOR WHICH YOU ARE COMPLETELY RESPONSIBLE.

IF YOU DON'T DO IT, IT DOESN'T GET DONE.

KEY RESULT AREAS ARE SIMILAR TO THE VITAL FUNCTIONS OF THE BODY, SUCH AS THOSE INDICATED BY BLOOD PRESSURE, HEART RATE, RESPIRATORY RATE, AND BRAINWAVE ACTIVITY.

AN ABSENCE OF ANY ONE OF THESE VITAL FUNCTIONS LEADS TO THE DEATH OF THE ORGANISM.

BY THE SAME TOKEN, YOUR FAILURE TO PERFORM IN A CRITICAL RESULT AREA OF YOUR WORK CAN LEAD TO THE END OF YOUR JOB.

THE STARTING POINT OF HIGH-PERFORMANCE IS FOR YOU TO IDENTIFY THE KEY RESULT AREAS OF YOUR WORK.

DISCUSS THEM WITH YOUR BOSS.

PRESIDENT

VP MARKETING

VP SALES

MANAGER

MANAGER

MANAGER

MAKE A LIST OF YOUR MOST IMPORTANT OUTPUT RESPONSIBILITIES, AND MAKE SURE THAT THE PEOPLE ABOVE YOU, ON THE SAME LEVEL AS YOU, AND BELOW YOU ARE IN AGREEMENT WITH IT.

ONCE YOU HAVE DETERMINED YOUR KEY RESULT AREAS, THE SECOND STEP IS FOR YOU TO GRADE YOURSELF ON A SCALE OF ONE TO TEN IN EACH OF THOSE AREAS.

A+

WHERE ARE YOU STRONG, AND WHERE ARE YOU WEAK?

YOUR WEAKEST KEY RESULT AREA SETS THE HEIGHT AT WHICH YOU CAN USE ALL YOUR OTHER SKILLS AND ABILITIES.

$0 + 0 = ?$

THIS RULE SAYS THAT ALTHOUGH YOU COULD BE EXCEPTIONAL IN SIX OUT OF SEVEN KEY RESULT AREAS, POOR PERFORMANCE IN THE SEVENTH AREA WILL HOLD YOU BACK.

HERE IS ONE OF THE GREATEST QUESTIONS YOU'LL EVER ASK AND ANSWER:

WHAT ONE SKILL, IF I DEVELOPED AND DID IT IN AN EXCELLENT FASHION, WOULD HAVE THE GREATEST POSITIVE IMPACT ON MY CAREER?

ASK YOUR BOSS THE QUESTION.

ASK YOUR FRIENDS AND FAMILY.

ASK YOUR COWORKERS.

LOOK INTO YOURSELF FOR THE ANSWER.

YOU PROBABLY *KNOW* WHAT IT IS.

WHATEVER THE ANSWER IS, FIND OUT AND THEN WORK TO BRING UP YOUR PERFORMANCE IN THIS AREA

ONE OF THE FASTEST AND BEST WAYS TO GET MORE THINGS DONE FASTER IS FOR YOU TO BECOME ABSOLUTELY EXCELLENT IN YOUR KEY RESULT AREAS.

THERE ARE THREE CORE TASKS YOU PERFORM THAT CONTAIN MOST OF THE VALUE YOU CONTRIBUTE TO YOUR BUSINESS OR ORGANIZATION.

ASK YOUR COWORKERS.

YOUR ABILITY TO ACCURATELY IDENTIFY THESE THREE KEY TASKS AND THEN FOCUS ON THEM MOST OF THE TIME IS **ESSENTIAL** FOR YOU TO PERFORM AT YOUR BEST.

DETERMINE THE THREE MOST IMPORTANT TASKS YOU DO IN YOUR WORK BY ASKING YOURSELF...

IF I COULD DO ONLY ONE TASK ALL DAY LONG, WHAT WOULD CONTRIBUTE THE GREATEST VALUE TO MY CAREER?

ONCE YOU HAVE IDENTIFIED YOUR "BIG THREE," CONCENTRATE ON THEM SINGLE-MINDEDLY FOR AN ENTIRE DAY.

IDENTIFY YOUR THREE MOST IMPORTANT GOALS IN EACH AREA OF YOUR LIFE.

ORGANIZE THEM BY PRIORITY.

MAKE PLANS FOR THEIR ACCOMPLISHMENT, AND WORK ON YOUR PLANS EVERY SINGLE DAY.

YOU WILL BE AMAZED AT WHAT YOU CAN ACHIEVE IN THE MONTHS AND YEARS AHEAD.

BEGIN BY CLEARING OFF YOUR DESK OR WORKSPACE SO YOU HAVE ONLY ONE TASK IN FRONT OF YOU.

IF NECESSARY, PUT EVERYTHING ON THE FLOOR OR ON A TABLE BEHIND YOU.

GATHER ALL THE INFORMATION, REPORTS, DETAILS, PAPERS, AND WORK MATERIALS YOU WILL REQUIRE TO COMPLETE THE JOB.

HAVE MATERIALS CLOSE AT HAND SO YOU CAN REACH THEM WITHOUT GETTING UP OR MOVING MUCH.

THE MOST PRODUCTIVE PEOPLE TAKE THE TIME TO CREATE A WORK AREA WHERE THEY ENJOY SPENDING TIME.

MAKE YOUR WORK AREA COMFORTABLE, ATTRACTIVE, AND CONDUCIVE TO WORKING FOR LONG PERIODS.

THE CLEANER AND NEATER YOUR WORK AREA *BEFORE YOU BEGIN,* THE EASIER IT WILL BE FOR YOU TO GET STARTED AND *KEEP GOING.*

IT IS AMAZING HOW MANY BOOKS NEVER GET WRITTEN, HOW MANY DEGREES NEVER GET COMPLETED, HOW MANY LIFE-CHANGING TASKS NEVER GET STARTED...

...SIMPLY BECAUSE PEOPLE FAIL TO TAKE THE FIRST STEP OF PREPARING EVERYTHING IN ADVANCE.

LOS ANGELES ATTRACTS PEOPLE FROM ALL OVER WHO DREAM OF WRITING A SUCCESSFUL MOVIE SCRIPT AND SELLING IT TO ONE OF THE STUDIOS.

HOLLYWOOD

THE LOS ANGELES TIMES ONCE SENT A REPORTER OUT ONTO WILSHIRE BOULEVARD TO INTERVIEW PASSERSBY.

HOW'S YOUR SCRIPT COMING?

THREE OUT OF FOUR PASSERSBY REPLIED...

ALMOST DONE!

PRESS

THE SAD FACT IS THAT "ALMOST DONE" PROBABLY MEANT "NOT YET STARTED."

DON'T LET THIS HAPPEN TO YOU.

SCENE ONE,

ONCE YOU HAVE COMPLETED YOUR PREPARATIONS, IT IS ESSENTIAL YOU LAUNCH IMMEDIATELY TOWARD YOUR GOALS.

GET STARTED. DO THE FIRST THING, WHATEVER IT IS.

MY PERSONAL RULE IS "GET IT 80% RIGHT AND CORRECT IT LATER."

DON'T EXPECT PERFECTION THE FIRST TIME OR EVEN THE FIRST FEW TIMES. BE PREPARED TO FAIL OVER AND OVER BEFORE YOU GET IT RIGHT.

THE ONLY WAY TO OVERCOME YOUR FEAR IS TO "DO THE THING YOU FEAR," AS EMERSON WROTE, "AND THE DEATH OF FEAR IS CERTAIN."

WAYNE GRETZKY, THE GREAT HOCKEY PLAYER, ONCE SAID...

YOU MISS 100% OF THE SHOTS YOU DON'T TAKE.

ONCE YOU HAVE COMPLETED YOUR PREPARATIONS, HAVE THE COURAGE TO TAKE THE FIRST ACTION!

EVERYTHING ELSE WILL FOLLOW FROM THAT.

ONE OF THE BEST WAYS TO OVERCOME PROCRASTINATION IS TO GET YOUR MIND OFF THE HUGE TASK IN FRONT OF YOU...

...AND INSTEAD FOCUS ON A SINGLE ACTION YOU **CAN** TAKE.

ONE OF THE BEST WAYS TO EAT A LARGE FROG IS FOR YOU TO DO IT ONE BITE AT A TIME.

LAO-TZU WROTE, "A JOURNEY OF 1,000 LEAGUES BEGINS WITH A SINGLE STEP."

MANY YEARS AGO, DRIVING AN OLD LAND ROVER, I CROSSED THE HEART OF THE SAHARA DESERT.

THE DESERT WAS 500 MILES ACROSS IN A SINGLE STRETCH, WITHOUT WATER, FOOD, A BLADE OF GRASS, OR EVEN A FLY.

MORE THAN 1,300 PEOPLE HAD PERISHED IN THE CROSSING OF THAT STRETCH OF THE SAHARA IN PREVIOUS YEARS.

OFTEN, THE DRIFTING SAND HAD OBLITERATED THE TRACK ACROSS THE DESERT, AND THE TRAVELERS GOT LOST IN THE NIGHT, NEVER TO BE FOUND AGAIN ALIVE.

38

TO COUNTER THIS LACK OF FEATURES IN THE TERRAIN, FRENCH TRAVELERS HAD MARKED THE TRACK WITH BLACK, 55-GALLON OIL DRUMS EVERY FIVE KILOMETERS.
THAT WAS ALL WE NEEDED TO STAY ON COURSE.
ALL WE HAD TO DO WAS STEER FOR THE NEXT OIL BARREL.
AS A RESULT, WE WERE ABLE TO CROSS THE BIGGEST DESERT IN THE WORLD BY SIMPLY TAKING IT "ONE BARREL AT A TIME."
SELECT ANY GOAL, TASK, OR PROJECT IN YOUR LIFE ON WHICH YOU HAVE BEEN PROCRASTINATING...
...AND MAKE A LIST OF ALL THE STEPS YOU WILL NEED TO TAKE TO EVENTUALLY COMPLETE THE TASK.
THEN TAKE JUST ONE STEP *IMMEDIATELY*.

ONE OF YOUR GREAT RESPONSIBILITIES IN LIFE IS TO DECIDE FOR YOURSELF WHAT YOU REALLY LOVE TO DO...

...AND THEN TO THROW YOUR WHOLE HEART INTO DOING THAT SPECIAL THING VERY, VERY WELL.

SUCCESSFUL PEOPLE ARE INVARIABLY THOSE WHO HAVE TAKEN THE TIME TO IDENTIFY WHAT THEY DO WELL AND MOST ENJOY.

YOU CANNOT DO EVERYTHING, BUT YOU **CAN** DO THOSE THINGS AT WHICH YOU EXCEL.

BETWEEN WHERE YOU ARE TODAY AND ANY GOAL YOU WANT TO ACCOMPLISH, THERE IS ONE MAJOR CONSTRAINT THAT MUST BE OVERCOME BEFORE YOU CAN ACHIEVE SAID GOAL.

YOUR JOB IS TO IDENTIFY IT CLEARLY.

WHAT IS HOLDING YOU BACK?

WHAT SETS THE SPEED AT WHICH YOU CAN ACHIEVE YOUR GOALS?

WHATEVER YOU HAVE TO DO, THERE IS ALWAYS A LIMITING FACTOR THAT DETERMINES HOW QUICKLY AND HOW WELL YOU GET IT DONE.

IN VIRTUALLY EVERY TASK, A SINGLE FACTOR SETS THE SPEED AT WHICH YOU ACHIEVE THE GOAL.

CONCENTRATE YOUR MENTAL ENERGIES ON THAT ONE KEY AREA.

THIS CONSTRAINT MAY BE A PERSON WHOSE HELP YOU NEED, A RESOURCE YOU REQUIRE, A WEAKNESS IN SOME PART OF THE ORGANIZATION, OR SOMETHING ELSE.

BUT THE LIMITING FACTOR IS ALWAYS THERE, AND IT IS ALWAYS YOUR JOB TO FIND IT.

STARTING OFF YOUR DAY WITH THE REMOVAL OF A KEY BOTTLENECK OR CONSTRAINT FILLS YOU WITH ENERGY AND PERSONAL POWER.

ONE OF THE BEST WAYS TO OVERCOME PROCRASTINATION IS BY WORKING AS THOUGH YOU HAVE ONLY ONE DAY TO GET YOUR MOST IMPORTANT JOBS DONE.

IMAGINE YOU JUST RECEIVED AN ALL EXPENSES PAID VACATION TO A BEAUTIFUL RESORT...

...BUT YOU WILL HAVE TO LEAVE TOMORROW MORNING OR THE VACATION WILL BE GIVEN TO SOMEONE ELSE.

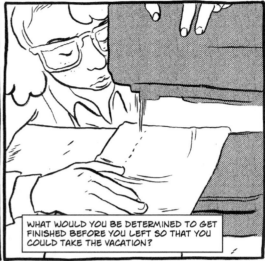

WHAT WOULD YOU BE DETERMINED TO GET FINISHED BEFORE YOU LEFT SO THAT YOU COULD TAKE THE VACATION?

WHATEVER IT IS, START ON THAT ONE JOB *IMMEDIATELY.*

45

ACCORDING TO MANY RESEARCHERS, THE AVERAGE AMERICAN DOES NOT GET ENOUGH SLEEP RELATIVE TO THE AMOUNT OF WORK HE OR SHE PERFORMS.

ONE OF THE SMARTEST THINGS YOU CAN DO IS TO TURN OFF THE TELEVISION AND GET TO BED BY 10 PM EACH NIGHT DURING THE WEEK.

SOMETIMES ONE EXTRA HOUR OF SLEEP PER NIGHT CAN CHANGE YOUR ENTIRE LIFE.

TAKE ONE FULL DAY OFF EVERY WEEK.

DURING THIS DAY, ABSOLUTELY REFUSE TO READ, CLEAR CORRESPONDENCE, CATCH UP ON THINGS FROM THE OFFICE, OR DO ANYTHING ELSE THAT TAXES YOUR BRAIN.

INSTEAD, WATCH A MOVIE, EXERCISE, SPEND TIME WITH YOUR FAMILY, TAKE A WALK -- PARTICIPATE IN ANY ACTIVITY THAT ALLOWS YOUR BRAIN TO COMPLETELY RECHARGE ITSELF.

TAKE REGULAR VACATIONS EACH YEAR, BOTH LONG WEEKENDS AND ONE AND TWO WEEK BREAKS, TO REST AND REJUVENATE.

TO PERFORM AT YOUR BEST, YOU MUST BECOME YOUR OWN PERSONAL CHEERLEADER.

YOU MUST DEVELOP A ROUTINE OF COACHING YOURSELF AND ENCOURAGING YOURSELF TO PLAY AT THE TOP OF YOUR GAME.

MOST OF YOUR EMOTIONS, POSITIVE OR NEGATIVE, ARE DETERMINED BY HOW YOU TALK TO YOURSELF ON A MINUTE-TO-MINUTE BASIS.

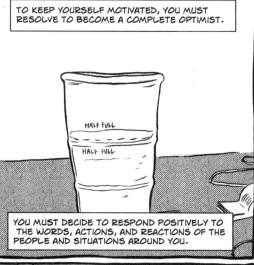

TO KEEP YOURSELF MOTIVATED, YOU MUST RESOLVE TO BECOME A COMPLETE OPTIMIST.

HALF FULL

HALF FULL

YOU MUST DECIDE TO RESPOND POSITIVELY TO THE WORDS, ACTIONS, AND REACTIONS OF THE PEOPLE AND SITUATIONS AROUND YOU.

YOU MUST REFUSE TO LET THE UNAVOIDABLE DIFFICULTIES AND SETBACKS OF DAILY LIFE AFFECT YOUR MOOD OR EMOTIONS.

TECHNOLOGY CAN BE YOUR BEST FRIEND...

...OR YOUR WORST ENEMY.

THE COMPULSION TO COMMUNICATE INCESSANTLY...

...THE NONSTOP USE OF EMAIL, CELL PHONES, THE INTERNET, AND VARIOUS CONTACT MANAGEMENT SYSTEMS...

...TENDS TO LEAVE PEOPLE PSYCHOLOGICALLY BREATHLESS.

WE HAVE NO TIME TO STOP, SMELL THE ROSES, AND COLLECT OUR THOUGHTS.

TO STAY CALM, CLEAR HEADED, AND CAPABLE OF PERFORMING AT YOUR BEST...

...DETACH YOURSELF FROM TECHNOLOGY AND COMMUNICATION DEVICES ON A REGULAR BASIS...

...BECAUSE THEY CAN OVERWHELM YOU IF YOU ARE NOT CAREFUL.

RESOLVE TODAY TO CREATE ZONES OF SILENCE DURING YOUR DAY-TO-DAY ACTIVITIES.

TURN OFF COMMUNICATION DEVICES AND TECHNOLOGY FOR ONE HOUR IN THE MORNING AND ONE HOUR IN THE AFTERNOON.

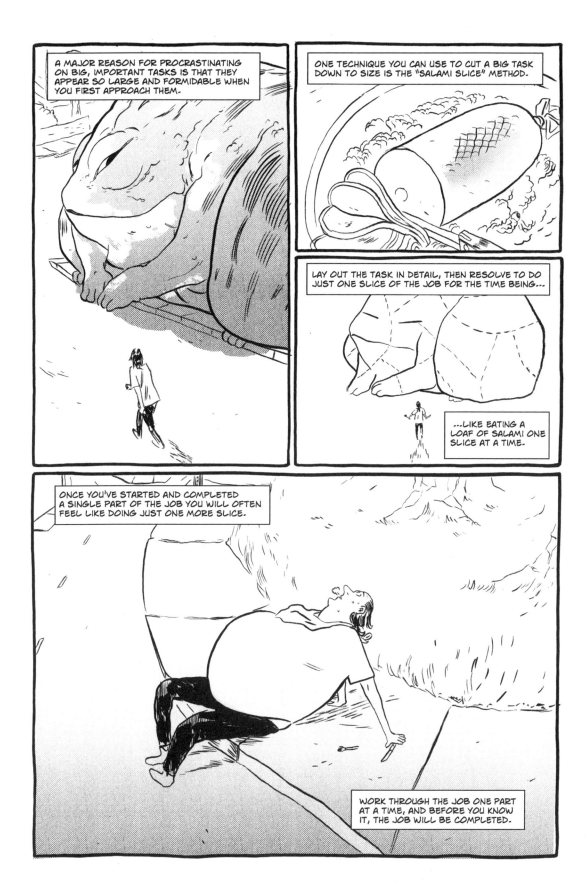

A MAJOR REASON FOR PROCRASTINATING ON BIG, IMPORTANT TASKS IS THAT THEY APPEAR SO LARGE AND FORMIDABLE WHEN YOU FIRST APPROACH THEM.

ONE TECHNIQUE YOU CAN USE TO CUT A BIG TASK DOWN TO SIZE IS THE "SALAMI SLICE" METHOD.

LAY OUT THE TASK IN DETAIL, THEN RESOLVE TO DO JUST ONE SLICE OF THE JOB FOR THE TIME BEING...

...LIKE EATING A LOAF OF SALAMI ONE SLICE AT A TIME.

ONCE YOU'VE STARTED AND COMPLETED A SINGLE PART OF THE JOB YOU WILL OFTEN FEEL LIKE DOING JUST ONE MORE SLICE.

WORK THROUGH THE JOB ONE PART AT A TIME, AND BEFORE YOU KNOW IT, THE JOB WILL BE COMPLETED.

MOST OF THE REALLY IMPORTANT WORK YOU DO REQUIRES LARGE CHUNKS OF UNBROKEN TIME TO COMPLETE.

YOUR ABILITY TO CARVE OUT AND USE THESE BLOCKS OF HIGH-VALUE, HIGHLY PRODUCTIVE TIME IS CENTRAL TO MAKING A SIGNIFICANT CONTRIBUTION TO YOUR WORK.

SUNDAY

MONDAY

SUNDAY

MONDAY

PLAN YOUR DAY IN ADVANCE, AND SCHEDULE A FIXED TIME PERIOD FOR A PARTICULAR ACTIVITY OR TASK.

MAKE WORK APPOINTMENTS WITH YOURSELF, AND DISCIPLINE YOURSELF TO KEEP THEM.

SET ASIDE THIRTY-, SIXTY-, AND NINETY-MINUTE TIME SEGMENTS THAT YOU USE TO WORK ON, AND COMPLETE, IMPORTANT TASKS.

DO NOT DISTURB

WHEN YOU FLY ON BUSINESS YOU CAN CREATE YOUR OFFICE IN THE AIR BY PLANNING YOUR WORK THOROUGHLY BEFORE DEPARTURE.

YOU CAN THEN WORK NONSTOP FOR THE ENTIRE FLIGHT.

YOU WILL BE AMAZED AT HOW MUCH YOU CAN GET DONE WHEN YOU WORK STEADILY IN AN AIRPLANE WITHOUT INTERRUPTIONS.

ONE OF THE KEYS TO HIGH LEVELS OF PERFORMANCE AND PRODUCTIVITY IS TO MAKE EVERY MINUTE COUNT.

PERHAPS THE MOST OUTWARDLY IDENTIFIABLE QUALITY OF HIGH-PERFORMING MEN AND WOMEN IS *ACTION ORIENTATION.*

THEY ARE IN A HURRY TO GET THEIR TASKS COMPLETED.

HIGHLY PRODUCTIVE PEOPLE TAKE THE TIME TO THINK, PLAN, AND SET PRIORITIES.

THEY THEN LAUNCH QUICKLY AND STRONGLY TOWARD THEIR GOALS AND OBJECTIVES.

WHEN YOU WORK ON THE MOST IMPORTANT TASKS AT A HIGH AND CONTINUOUS LEVEL OF ACTIVITY, YOU ENTER INTO AN AMAZING MENTAL STATE CALLED *"FLOW."*

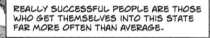

REALLY SUCCESSFUL PEOPLE ARE THOSE WHO GET THEMSELVES INTO THIS STATE FAR MORE OFTEN THAN AVERAGE.

ONE OF THE WAYS YOU CAN TRIGGER THIS STATE OF FLOW IS BY DEVELOPING A SENSE OF URGENCY.

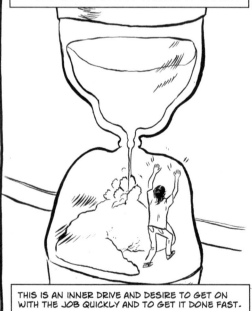

THIS IS AN INNER DRIVE AND DESIRE TO GET ON WITH THE JOB QUICKLY AND TO GET IT DONE FAST.

RESOLVE TODAY TO DEVELOP A SENSE OF URGENCY IN EVERYTHING YOU DO.

CONSIDER AN AREA WHERE YOU HAVE A TENDENCY TO PROCRASTINATE, AND DEVELOP THE HABIT OF *FAST ACTION* IN THAT AREA.

EAT THAT FROG!

EVERY BIT OF PLANNING, PRIORITIZING, AND ORGANIZING COMES DOWN TO THIS SIMPLE CONCEPT.

YOUR ABILITY TO SELECT YOUR MOST IMPORTANT TASK, TO BEGIN IT, AND THEN TO CONCENTRATE ON IT SINGLE-MINDEDLY UNTIL IT IS COMPLETE...

...IS THE KEY TO HIGH LEVELS OF PERFORMANCE AND PERSONAL PRODUCTIVITY.

ONCE YOU START YOUR MOST IMPORTANT TASK, DISCIPLINE YOURSELF TO PERSEVERE WITHOUT DIVERSION OR DISTRACTION UNTIL IT IS COMPLETE.

SEE IT AS A TEST TO DETERMINE WHETHER YOU'RE THE KIND OF PERSON WHO CAN MAKE A DECISION TO COMPLETE SOMETHING AND THEN CARRY IT OUT.

THE KEY TO HAPPINESS, SATISFACTION, SUCCESS, AND PERSONAL POWER IS TO DEVELOP THE HABIT OF EATING YOUR FROG FIRST THING EVERY DAY WHEN YOU START WORK.

FORTUNATELY, THIS IS A LEARNABLE SKILL THAT YOU CAN ACQUIRE THROUGH REPETITION.

ON THE FOLLOWING PAGES IS A SUMMARY OF SOME GREAT WAYS TO STOP PROCRASTINATING AND GET MORE DONE FASTER.

REVIEW THESE RULES AND PRINCIPLES REGULARLY UNTIL THEY BECOME FIRMLY INGRAINED IN YOUR THINKING AND ACTIONS, AND YOUR FUTURE WILL BE GUARANTEED.

SET THE TABLE.

DECIDE EXACTLY WHAT YOU WANT.

PLAN EVERY DAY IN ADVANCE.

THINK ON PAPER.

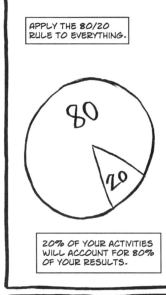

APPLY THE 80/20 RULE TO EVERYTHING.

20% OF YOUR ACTIVITIES WILL ACCOUNT FOR 80% OF YOUR RESULTS.

CONSIDER THE CONSEQUENCES.

YOUR MOST IMPORTANT TASKS AND PRIORITIES ARE THOSE THAT CAN HAVE THE MOST SERIOUS CONSEQUENCES.

PRACTICE CREATIVE PROCRASTINATION.

SINCE YOU CAN'T DO EVERYTHING, YOU MUST LEARN TO DELIBERATELY PUT OFF TASKS OF LOW VALUE.

USE THE ABCDE METHOD CONTINUALLY.

BEFORE YOU BEGIN WORK ON A LIST OF TASKS, TAKE A FEW MOMENTS TO ORGANIZE THEM BY VALUE AND PRIORITY.

FOCUS ON KEY RESULT AREAS.

IDENTIFY THE THREE THINGS YOU DO IN YOUR WORK THAT ACCOUNT FOR 90% OF YOUR CONTRIBUTION, AND FOCUS ON GETTING THEM DONE BEFORE ANYTHING ELSE.

PREPARE THOROUGHLY BEFORE YOU BEGIN.

HAVE EVERYTHING YOU NEED AT HAND BEFORE YOU START.

TAKE IT ONE OIL BARREL AT A TIME.

YOU CAN ACCOMPLISH THE BIGGEST AND MOST COMPLICATED JOB ONE STEP AT A TIME.

UPGRADE YOUR KEY SKILLS.

THE MORE KNOWLEDGEABLE AND SKILLED YOU BECOME AT YOUR KEY TASKS, THE FASTER YOU START THEM -- AND THE SOONER YOU GET THEM DONE.

LEVERAGE YOUR SPECIAL TALENTS.

DETERMINE WHAT YOU ARE VERY GOOD AT, OR COULD BE VERY GOOD AT, AND THROW YOUR WHOLE HEART INTO DOING THOSE SPECIFIC THINGS VERY WELL.

IDENTIFY YOUR KEY CONSTRAINTS.

DETERMINE THE BOTTLENECKS OR CHOKEPOINTS, INTERNAL OR EXTERNAL, THAT SET THE SPEED AT WHICH YOU ACHIEVE YOUR MOST IMPORTANT GOALS -- AND FOCUS ON ALLEVIATING THEM.

About the Author

Author and personal development expert Brian Tracy began his career in management consulting, real estate, and sales and marketing. He later founded his own firm, Brian Tracy International. His series of lectures on personal and professional development draw over 250,000 people each year.

About the Artist

Paul Maybury is an Award-winning artist and writer whose work has been featured by Marvel, DC, Dark Horse, Heavy Metal, Ubisoft, Metro, Image, Criterion and Mirage Studios. He lives in Austin, Texas.

THE BOOK THAT INSPIRED THE COMIC

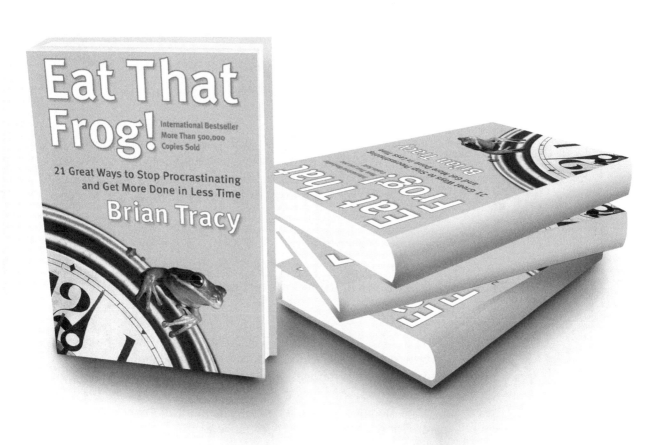

AVAILABLE EVERYWHERE
BOOKS ARE SOLD

Other titles from
SmarterComics®

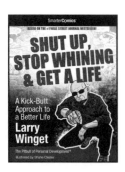

SHUT UP, STOP WHINING & GET A LIFE
from SmarterComics

by Larry Winget

Internationally renowned success philosopher, business speaker, and humorist, Larry Winget offers advice that flies in the face of conventional self-help. SHUT UP, STOP WHINING, AND GET A LIFE forces all responsibility for every aspect of your life right where it belongs: on you.

THE ART OF WAR from SmarterComics

by Sun Tzu

Written by an ancient Chinese military general and philosopher, THE ART OF WAR reveals the subtle secrets of successful competition – equally applicable to war, business, politics, sports, law, poker, gaming, and life. Required reading in modern business schools!

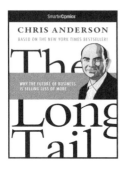

THE LONG TAIL from SmarterComics

by Chris Anderson

Now in comic format, this 2006 New York Times bestseller introduced the business world to a future that's already here. It explains why the focus of Internet commerce is not on hits but on misses-the long tail of the demand curve – and illuminates the reasons behind the success of niche operations like Amazon. com, iTunes, and Netflix. A must-read for every entrepreneur and manager.

OVERACHIEVEMENT from SmarterComics

by Dr. John Eliot

In OVERACHIEVEMENT from SmarterComics, Dr. Eliot offers the rest of us the unconventional and counterintuitive concepts embraced by Olympic athletes, business moguls, rock stars, top surgeons, salespeople, and financial experts who have turned to him for performance-enhancement advice.

Other titles from
SmarterComics®

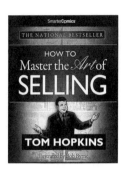

HOW TO MASTER THE ART OF SELLING
from SmarterComics

by Tom Hopkins

A national bestseller, with over one million copies sold in its original version, this book is a classic for teaching the tools of selling success. Lauded by motivational icon Zig Ziglar, the author has been called "America's #1 sales trainer."

FORTUNE FAVORS THE BOLD from SmarterComics

by Franco Arda

Written by the founder of SmarterComics, this powerful little manual packs a punch. If you want to grab life by the horns but tend to drag your feet doing it, this comic is for you.

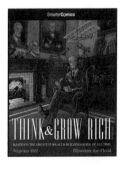

THINK & GROW RICH from SmarterComics

by Napoleon Hill

Want to learn the principles of getting rich in less than an hour? Take the illustrated advice of millionaire Andrew Carnegie, whose observations make up the heart of the best-selling classic "Think and Grow Rich." Now updated into an engaging comic book format, you can quickly glean Carnegie's wisdom from these beautifully illustrated panels.

THE BOOK OF 5 RINGS from SmarterComics

by Miyamoto Musashi

Infamous 17th century samurai Miyamoto Musashi (1584-1645) never lost a fight. His unprecedented winning streak wasn't based on supernatural powers: he was a keen master of strategy, timing, and the nuances of human interaction. He recorded his brilliant observations in „The Book of Five Rings" in 1643.

FREE GIFTS

Download Brian Tracy's Eat That Frog Mp3 and Teleseminar Notes for FREE!

To receive your FREE gifts, go to:

www.BrianTracy.com/FrogGift

Sign up for Brian Tracy's Time Management Newsletter and receive a Free Mp3 download of Eat That Frog! and the PDF notes to go along with it.

Isn't it time you learned how get more done in less time? Once you become a Master of Time your stress load will decrease dramatically and you'll have more time to actually do the things you really enjoy in life.

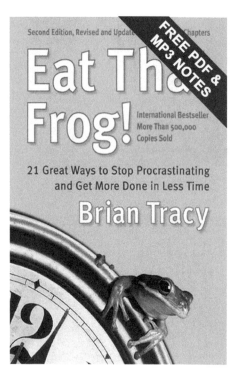

In this newsletter you'll learn how to:

• Organize your tasks and priorities

• Get more done in less time with better time management

• Develop efficient organization skills and increase productivity

• Relieve stress and create work life balance

Did you know that improving in only one area of your life could help you manage your time, and improve your success in life? Do you want to know what this one area of YOUR personal life is?

Now with the help of Brian Tracy's Time Management assessment you will quickly diagnose your time management activities in 30 different areas. You'll discover your strengths, weaknesses, threats and opportunities in less than 10 minutes of your time.

Once you submit your answers, you will receive a complete report on your time management skills with detailed instructions for the specific actions you can take to get more done in less time.

Brian Tracy has used this same exact tool to consult and help thousands of people over the last 30 years, and now it's my gift to you for FREE.

To take this FREE assessment, go to:

www.BrianTracy.com/FrogTest

HOW TO MASTER YOUR TIME IPHONE APPLICATION

Success expert Brian Tracy has discovered the simple solution to time mastery and it doesn't mean letting the clock rule your life.

In fact, the very opposite is true: time mastery will give you the absolute freedom to do what you want, when you want to do it.

With 20 years of research and experience in the subject, Brian Tracy has created a program that will teach you the philosophy of time management, how to internalize it, and show you how to develop a belief system that will make your every moment more efficient.

Through repeated listening to these tracks, you'll learn how to:

• Visualize efficiency and excellence using mental rehearsal techniques

• Lead others as an example of successful time management

• Become results-oriented, working smarter, not harder

• Delegate more effectively and become more adept at prioritizing

• Energize yourself with the positive results of your labor

To download the How to Master Your Time application, go to:

www.BrianTracy.com/TimeApp

EAT THAT FROG IPHONE APPLICATION

The key to reaching high levels of performance and productivity is to develop the lifelong habit of tackling your major task first thing each morning. You must develop the routine of "eating your frog" before you do anything else, and without taking too much time to think about it.

Brian Tracy's Eat That Frog iPhone application has been specifically designed and developed to ensure that your biggest priorities are handled with the urgency and focus required to make you most effective in your business and personal life.

Each day, you'll be impressed with the momentum created from tackling your most difficult tasks and at the end of each week and month you'll be amazed to see just how much you've completed!

Application Features:

• Establish as many custom "frogs" as you like

• Track your daily Frog and add required steps t keep you on target

• Chart both completions percentages and status

• Email chart data directly from app

• Plus much more!

To download the Eat That Frog application, go to:

www.BrianTracy.com/FrogApp

EAT THAT FROG

for iPhone, Pad, Kindle or Android

Berrett–Koehler
Publishers

Berrett-Koehler is an independent publisher dedicated to an ambitious mission: *Creating a World That Works for All.*

We believe that to truly create a better world, action is needed at all levels—individual, organizational, and societal. At the individual level, our publications help people align their lives with their values and with their aspirations for a better world. At the organizational level, our publications promote progressive leadership and management practices, socially responsible approaches to business, and humane and effective organizations. At the societal level, our publications advance social and economic justice, shared prosperity, sustainability, and new solutions to national and global issues.

A major theme of our publications is "Opening Up New Space." Berrett-Koehler titles challenge conventional thinking, introduce new ideas, and foster positive change. Their common quest is changing the underlying beliefs, mindsets, institutions, and structures that keep generating the same cycles of problems, no matter who our leaders are or what improvement programs we adopt.

We strive to practice what we preach—to operate our publishing company in line with the ideas in our books. At the core of our approach is stewardship, which we define as a deep sense of responsibility to administer the company for the benefit of all of our "stakeholder" groups: authors, customers, employees, investors, service providers, and the communities and environment around us.

We are grateful to the thousands of readers, authors, and other friends of the company who consider themselves to be part of the "BK Community." We hope that you, too, will join us in our mission.

A BK Life Book

This book is part of our BK Life series. BK Life books change people's lives. They help individuals improve their lives in ways that are beneficial for the families, organizations, communities, nations, and world in which they live and work. To find out more, visit **www.bk-life.com**.

QUIZ

Q.1 What is the critical determinant of what you can accomplish?

a) Wealth and social standing.

b) Your ability to set priorities and act on these priorities.

c) Your ability to impress your friends, family, and employer.

Q.2 Who said this: "If the first thing you do each morning is to eat a live frog... you can go through the day knowing that that is probably the worst thing that is going to happen to you all day long"?

a) Benjamin Franklin.

b) Mohandes Ghandi.

c) Mark Twain.

Q.3 If you are faced with two important tasks, you should:

a) Work on them simultaneously.

b) Break each of the tasks down into smaller components and work on the individual pieces as time allows.

c) Start with the biggest, hardest, and most important of the two tasks

Q.4 You can increase your productivity and output by 25 percent or more from the first day that you:

a) Begin consistently working from a list.

b) Begin delegating your most important tasks.

c) Begin saying "no" to new assignments.

Q.5 You should work from the following lists:

a) A monthly task list.

b) A monthly and weekly task list.

c) A master task list, a monthly task list, a weekly task list, and a daily task list.

Q.6 Time management is really:

a) Life management.

b) Resource management.

c) Impossible.

Q.7 Once you have completed your preparations for a project, it is essential that you:

a) Launch immediately toward your goals and begin work.

b) Track your time spent on each component of your project.

c) Validate your preparations with an educated third party.

Q.8 The 80/20 Rule states that:

a) 20% of your activities will account for 80% of your results.

b) You must put in 20% more time at work than 80% of your co-workers in order to be successful.

c) 20% of the tasks associated with all projects are pointless.

Q.9 One of the best ways for you to overcome procrastination and get more things done faster is to:

a) Clear your mind before you begin work.

b) Have everything you need at hand before you begin.

c) Purchase project management software.

Q.10 Perhaps the most outwardly identifiable quality of high-performing men and women is:

a) Wealth. They are successful in business.

b) Work/life balance.

c) Action orientation. They are in a hurry to get their tasks completed.

Please visit www.smartercomics.com/quizzes for the answers and more quizzes.

www.SMARTERCOMICS.com